Turning a Negative into a Positive

Turning a Negative into a Positive:

101 Creative Tips for Saving Money and
Finding Financial Peace

Lisa L. Evans

authorHOUSE®

AuthorHouse™
1663 Liberty Drive
Bloomington, IN 47403
www.authorhouse.com
Phone: 1-800-839-8640

© 2012 by Lisa L. Evans All rights reserved.

No part of this book may be reproduced, stored in a retrieval system, or transmitted by any means without the written permission of the author.

Published by AuthorHouse   03/09/2012

ISBN: 978-1-4685-5965-1 (sc)
ISBN: 978-1-4685-5966-8 (e)

Library of Congress Control Number: 2012904060

Any people depicted in stock imagery provided by Thinkstock are models, and such images are being used for illustrative purposes only.
Certain stock imagery © Thinkstock.

This book is printed on acid-free paper.

Because of the dynamic nature of the Internet, any web addresses or links contained in this book may have changed since publication and may no longer be valid. The views expressed in this work are solely those of the author and do not necessarily reflect the views of the publisher, and the publisher hereby disclaims any responsibility for them.

Lisa Evans

Dedication

Loyalty, respect, and love to my husband and son.

Special Thanks:

To my husband, who inadvertently inspired my 101 creative saving tips.

To my mom, who, in my younger years, did the exact opposite of the examples in this book, but has blossomed into a successful manager of her finances.

To my mother-in-law, my personal editor-in-chief.

In Memory of:

Victor L. Dillbeck

I could write a million pages and still be unable to say just how much I love and miss him every single day

Contents

Acknowledgments ix

Introduction xi

Chapter 1   Home & Car 1

Chapter 2   Children & Family 17

Chapter 3   Shopping & Dining 25

Chapter 4   Miscellaneous 69

Acknowledgments

First, I thank God just for who he is. I also thank him for all that he has done, is doing, and will do in my life.

I thank many great family members and friends for allowing me to be the unique person that I am.

Introduction

At the beginning of our marriage my husband and I had two different philosophies about money and we often bumped heads about it. Mistakes were made and fingers were pointed, but we still stayed in the same position until we decided to stop fighting each other and fight against the force that tries to consistently separate you from your money everyday. Since deciding to work together we have reduced our debt greatly and are able to comfortably meet goals that we have created for ourselves and our family. We have less stress, peace of mind, financial security, and we use our money, time, and energy towards activities that benefit our household.

Throughout the years we have learned from our mistakes and even been able to teach others what we have learned. As I learned, I recognized that there were many self-help books that repeated the same 8-10 suggestions about finances to readers, but didn't really give many real life examples. I began to put together real life examples that I have used that have allowed me to be successful at making better use of my family's income and putting the created savings towards more positive investments.

Chapter 1

Tip #1: Consistently evaluate your insurance coverage.

You should evaluate your car insurance every six months to see if you qualify for lower payments due to an increase in your credit score, a previous moving violation going beyond the 3 or 5 year effective point, or a new discount offer available such as safe driver or multi-policy discounts.

You should also reevaluate and make changes immediately when your circumstances change such as deleting a driver, paying off a vehicle, or reducing coverage during off riding seasons for recreational vehicles.

Tip #2: Appeal your property taxes.

Don't take your property tax increases lying down. In this struggling economy everyone has their hand out for their portion of the pie. However, their portion may not be accurate and they should get less than they received before. Review your property tax bill and compare recent home sales in your immediate area and submit an application for appeal of your taxes if your taxes have increased and recent home sales show a consistent decline in value. Investing in a real estate or tax attorney can also save you time and money. They can use their experience and expertise to appeal your taxes and only bill you for a portion of the savings.

Tip #3: Preventative maintenance is cheaper than repairs.

This one is from my husband. He is adamant, strong-headed, and rightly-so about this tip. You should perform all of the recommended services and ongoing maintenance on all of your vehicles and large equipment such as furnaces and A/C units according to the equipment's listed maintenance plan. Proper and timely upkeep can prevent large repair bills in the future.

Tip #4: Paint.

You can pretty much paint anything; metal, wood, glass, fabric, etc. Paint is one of the cheapest ways of transforming an item or space. When you want to make a change you don't have to buy new, you can just paint it. In addition, one way to decorate without spending a lot of money would be to paint your walls or just one wall, better known as an "accent wall". One method of finding the right color for you is to gather several paint swatches from your local paint provider and tape them side-by-side on the wall you want to paint. View them during the day, midday, and at night. Slowly pull swatches down that do not view well until you narrow it down to your final one.

Tip #5: Buy pre-owned vehicles.

Well cared for pre-owned vehicles give the buyer the best bang for their buck. You can find almost every make, model, and year of a vehicle as a pre-owned vehicle. Be flexible on your color and trim and you can find a budget-friendly quality pre-owned vehicle with good equity.

Tip # 6: Use houseplants as décor.

Houseplants and small trees are inexpensive and make wonderful décor pieces. Whether they are real and faux they can be repotted in inexpensive colorful pots or urns and placed in corners to fill empty space. Additionally, adding a small spotlight behind a plant or tree can turn an ordinary plant into a designer look.

Tip #7: Bling Bling.

Mixing a little bling with something basic can create an overall look of glam. For example take a basic solid colored comforter set for a bed and add sparkly complimenting decorative pillows and you get a look of an expensive comforter set. The same goes for a basic outfit; add a little complimenting bling to it for extra pizzazz. However, be careful not to over bling.

Tip #8: Buy car parts from part stores.

Dealerships have large overhead and that has to be passed onto someone. That someone is you. The largest money makers at dealerships are parts and labor. Buy your certified car parts at part stores. Part stores carry most makes and models of car parts and they are often half the price of what you would pay at the dealership.

Tip #9: The world is a stage.

Whether you are selling your primary residence or an investment property invest in property staging for a greater return on your investment. Whether you reduce clutter and stage the property yourself or hire a professional you will get back the money you are investing plus some.

Tip #10: "Ride it until the wheels fall off."

-Martin Lawrence

If your car still works, keep driving it. If through proper care and reasonable maintenance your car gets you from point A to Point B then you should keep it. A new car brings a new payment, higher insurance, and an unnecessary pull from your savings.

Tip #11: Pay your mortgage bi-weekly.

Paying your mortgage bi-weekly helps break down your payment into a manageable amount, and pay down the mortgage sooner. If you have a mortgage payment of $1400 and you get paid bi-weekly, you can split this payment into two $700 payments, and by doing this you will actually make 1 additional principle payment per year which could result in you paying off your mortgage 5-7 years sooner.

Tip #12: Buy a home on one income.

Instead of maxing out the amount of home you can purchase based on two incomes, purchase a home based on the one larger income. You will be much more comfortable and in the event that one person is no longer working the mortgage can still be paid on one income.

Tip #13: Save on gas.

Use smart phone apps and even calls to friends or family to check current gas prices. If the drive for cheaper gas is within 2-3 miles you should take it for the greater savings. You may only save 5 cents per gallon on your one trip, but this savings adds up over the year for a larger impact.

Chapter 2

Tip #14: Pay your tithes.

No need to get wordy on this tip. Tithing is not an option, it's a Christian requirement. Tithe your 10% as well as sow seeds in other fertile places. I have found that paying our tithes saves money because when you pay your tithes you are doing two things. One, you are obeying God's word (and it will return to you overflowing) and two, you are following a budget. When you don't pay your tithes you end up spending the tithe money and even more money leaving you in a deeper hole than if you were to have just paid your tithes and kept your focus.

Tip #15: Visit friends and family often.

Visiting friends and family often helps keep these important relationships healthy; and the more time spent building the bonds of friendship and family the less time you will spend focusing on other less important things.

Tip #16: Public or private school.

Why pay twice for the same thing. Unless you live in an underfunded or underperforming school district you should use the public schools available to you. A large portion of your tax dollars goes to public education; therefore you should use the education that you are already paying for. With your attentiveness, and other free resources around you, your child can receive a quality education from the public school system.

Tip #17: Buy life insurance early.

Life insurance is absolutely necessary to make sure your final expenses are taken care of and your family is able to continue on financially in your absence. Buy term life insurance plans because they are cheaper than whole life and you are only paying for insurance if you need it. Term life has no cash value, and you only get the return on your investment if you were to become deceased. The earlier in life you purchase the coverage the lower the rates are. So buy it sooner rather than later. If your job offers you additional term life you should take it because they are getting a great group rate and they are able to offer the benefit to you for much cheaper than you could get it on your own.

Tip #18: Go petless.

Although dogs are known as man's best friend, and cats make good silent companions, pets can add to your monthly and yearly financial liabilities. All pets require a minimal amount of care, but more and more are requiring additional care through grooming, healthcare, and additional ownership expenses such as yearly pet registration or pet rent if you live in a rental unit.

Chapter 3

Tip #19: Shop at consignment stores.

Consignment and resale shops are different than thrift stores. Consignment and reliable resale shops are clean, tidy, and their items are pre-screened for spots, rips, and missing items such as buttons or snaps. You can find great brand name clothing and accessories at these stores. Often times you can also find items with tags still attached.

On one occasion a resale shop was having a sale. I was given a large grocery size paper bag, and whatever I could fit in the bag was $15. I managed to fit my son 8 pairs of pants and shorts, 12 shirts (rolled army style), 4 belts, 3 spring jackets into the bag. All of these items would have cost over $300 through retail stores.

Although consignment shops are tidier than thrift stores, wash all of your findings when you get them home.

Tip #20: Don't let your family see the bag.

Many off brands of many items ranging from clothing, cleaning supplies, food, and even home décor are identical to the brand name. And if it weren't for the tag on the item or the bag you carried it in with most people wouldn't know the difference.

Tip #21: Layaway is back. Use it.

Get over the stigma that layaway is for poor people who can't afford to buy an item outright or do not have good credit. Wrong! Layaway is a smart tool because it allows you to get the items you want and pay CASH in increments until it is paid off. This is a good thing because once the layaway is paid in full, and you pick up your items, there is no hardship involved in the purchase and the items aren't associated with any debt.

Tip #22: Repurpose items.

Many household items can be repurposed and used as something else. Empty wine bottles can be used as decoration on a dining room table or above your kitchen cabinets. Old picture frames can be gathered and used to make one large art piece on a wall. The list goes on and on.

Tip #23: Only buy in bulk when needed.

Do you have a membership to a large warehouse such as Costco or Sam's Club? These are great stores when you use them properly. Because items come in large quantities they can be easily wasted if not used in time, making the discount you received worthless. This is especially true for food products. However, household products such as trash bags, dish detergent, washing detergent, bathroom cleaner, and paper products are better items to purchase in bulk.

Tip #24: Buy used furniture.

When you need a piece of furniture such as a coffee table, sofa table, or sitting chair to fill a space in your home, search a consignment shop, used hotel furniture store, or garage sales. These places have unique or vintage pieces of furniture that make great additions to your space. For extra pizzazz wood furniture can be painted with high quality paint to match your other furniture or to add a pop of color to a space.

Tip #25: Share a meal.

American restaurants are known for their large portions compared to other countries. Take advantage of this and feel comfortable sharing a meal with a friend or partner. Some restaurants, if asked, will split the meal for you as it is being prepared to serve, and others you just have to ask for an extra plate or saucer. Split the meal, and you easily split the bill.

Tip #26: Drink water.

My young son always asks if he can have some juice. In return I ask him what he thinks I'm going to say. He pauses, but he always replies, "Drink water". He's absolutely right. Drink water. It's not only healthy; it will save you a great deal of money. Water is cheaper than sodas and juices. In addition, sodas and juices are some of restaurants highest markup items. They cost restaurants pennies on the dollar, but they mark them up by 300%. You can even order cups of water at the movie theater and save on your snack bill.

Tip #27: Faux is the way to go.

This is a favorite of my husband. He loves the fact that I love to accessorize with faux jewelry. When my spouse and I were dating he bought me a beautiful necklace with a gold and diamond heart locket. Although, I was thankful for the gift, I just kept thinking of how much faux accessories I could have gotten in place of the one gold necklace with a locket. Faux jewelry and accessories are a great way to get the glam look you are looking for without spending your child's college tuition.

Tip #28: Buy generic.

Do you think a guest would be able to tell if the green beans were brand name or store brand? Most guests can't tell the difference between brand name or store brand items. You can buy a number of items in generic or store brand and no one but yourself will know the difference between the two. Canned items, spices, condiments, paper products, lotions, mouthwash, aspirin, and antacid are great products to buy store brand.

Tip #29: Buy off-season for the holidays.

Black Friday, the day after Thanksgiving Day is not the only day after a holiday you can save big. The days following every holiday can bring you the best deals on holiday supplies. Everyone who knows me knows that I love to have parties (holiday parties, sport parties, birthday parties, etc) and entertain. What they don't know (but will after reading this tip) is that I buy most of my party supplies after the holidays where I get up to 75% off. In addition, throughout the year I find markdowns of 90% on discontinued designs and items. I have bought and decorated several beautiful parties for less than $20.

Tip #30: Mix brand names with off brands.

These days fashion doesn't follow one particular trend so you can be a little more flexible in brands. If you keep the logos and signatures to a minimum it is easy to mix the brands to get a great look.

Tip #31: Kids eat free.

In tip #25 you learned to share a meal with a friend or a spouse, and in tip #26 you learned to drink water with your meals. Now join that with Kids Eat Free meals. There are many restaurants that have Kids Eat Free meals with the purchase of an adult meal, or Kids Eat Free days. The average family of two adults and two kids can pay an average of $50 for dinner; but by combing these three tips the family can reduce the bill to an average $22.

Tip #32: Buy at thrift stores and resell.

Thrift stores are great places to find items that have resale value. Pre-owned wedding, bridesmaid, mother-of-the-bride, prom, and pageant dresses, pre-owned brand name sport shoes, and fur coats (yes, fur coats) have a large market on websites such as EBay.com and Amazon.com. Buy items on sale days for greater savings, and resell a little higher for a great side gig.

Tip #33: Buy less often.

One logical way to save money is to not go to the stores. Well if you have a family, large or small, this is next to impossible. But you can reduce how often you make trips to the stores, which reduces the likelihood of buying things you didn't intend to buy. Items that you can stock up on you should. Instead of buying one tube of toothpaste, one bottle of mouthwash, one container of lotion, one can of deodorant, one can of bathroom cleaner, etc, that will only last you 2-3 weeks, try buying 3-4 of the items at a time. You are actually spending less money on gas, and saving a lot of time (which is equal to money for many of us).

Tip #34: Use cash over credit.

Ever heard the old saying "cash is king"? Well it's true. You can get items for less money if you are willing to pay cash and you can also negotiate a better deal if you present cash on the spot. Studies also show that you spend less money if you are using cash over credit or debit cards because you visually see the cash leaving your hands, therefore you make wiser choices with it.

Tip #35: Eat appetizers.

Appetizers are less expensive than meals, and they are often just as large as a regular meal. Therefore, they can be ordered as your meal. Ask your server to bring it out as your meal.

Tip #36: Downgrade your dishware and flatware.

How often does someone compliment your spoons, forks, or plates? Usually never. Therefore, you do not have to spend a great deal of money on these eating utensils. Buy inexpensive dinnerware or flatware and add color or accessories with cloth napkins or sparkling placemats.

Tip #37: Complete surveys for discounts.

If a survey comes along with a discount, take the time to complete it. The 2-5 minutes to complete the survey could add up to real savings on your next visit. Limit taking surveys that do not have a savings benefit to you.

Tip #38: Take advantage of discount clubs.

Not only can you save by buying in bulk at discount clubs such as Costco or Sam's Club, you can save in areas such as gas discounts, vehicle tires, and even vacation packages. These clubs buy these and other items in bulk also and they are able to pass the savings onto you.

Tip #39: Skip extended warranties.

Stores offer you protection plans on everything from electronics to sporting goods. Eighty percent of the warranties are never used and they are a major profit for the vendor and the store selling them.

Tip #40: Get your rebate.

Retailers love when they offer a rebate to encourage you to buy their product and you don't redeem the rebate. Some retailers still use the mailing method of redeeming your retail, but many have updated their redemption method to receiving your rebate electronically. Either way, it only takes a few minutes to redeem your money. Don't let the retailers keep it.

Tip #41: Buy magazine subscriptions.

If you are like me, and love reading a magazine or two, then you should subscribe to them for 12 or 24 months. You will save substantially off the newsstand price and get the magazines 3-4 days before the newsstand.

Tip #42: Ask questions.

Most items on a menu or selection board are there because they are the most common products or services. They are also the products and services that providers make the most profit from. Do not be afraid to ask if there are other products or services to choose from. You can also ask if there are other less expensive options or other payment plans available. It doesn't cost anything to ask.

Tip #43: Check receipts and statements.

Almost 25% of the time there are errors and overcharges on your receipts or statements. Some of those errors or overcharges can be as small as a cent or two, but they can also be as large as a double or triple charge for a product or service. Checking your statements will also discover services charges that you are being billed because of a "passive reply". Meaning if you don't reply to the charge for the service, then you agree to accept the service and the charge. Cable and satellite providers are great at adding packages to your service and hoping you engage in the passive reply practice.

Tip #44: Buy greeting cards from discount stores.

Have you seen the cost of greeting cards lately? It could cost you more than $12 to say Happy Mother's Day to a mother and mother-in-law if you buy greeting cards at traditional stores. Buy greeting cards for as little as 2/$1.00 at discount retailers. If you want more creative wording or artistic features buy a box of occasion cards from membership retailers such as Costco or Sam's Club. You will get a box of 25-50 cards for various occasions that are decorative and classy for a great per unit price.

Tip #45: Use promotional codes.

Before you place an order online do a search for a promotional code. When you are on the checkout page of your shopping cart, many websites ask you if you have a promotional code to receive a discount. This discount may be a percentage off your total, a free or discounted item, or free shipping. Whatever the discount is, it is money in your pocket. Take a few extra minutes to search the internet for a promotional code to receive the discount. Many are found on the company's Facebook or Twitter pages, or on websites dedicated to finding promotional codes.

Tip #46: Buy your own snacks for road trips.

Whether traveling by plane, train, or automobile you should buy and pack your own snacks and even meals before your trip. Convenient store snacks and beverages along the way can be very expensive and could put a financial damper in your trip before you even get to your destination.

Tip #47: Make at least one weekend a month shop-free.

A shop-free weekend is a weekend free of unnecessary purchases and activities that you want rather than need. Cook your own meals, watch the cable you already pay for, or play board games or do outdoor activities (if the weather permits) that do not cost any money. If you master one weekend per month move onto 2 or 3 weekends per month.

Tip #48: Keep the hangers.

When you ask a retail store if you can keep the hangers, and you get either one of two responses, yes or no. If yes, this is great. Use the hangers to keep your closet organized, or to nicely display clothing you want to sell. There are hangers of all sorts, shirt, pant, coat, etc, ask to keep them when you are checking out.

Tip #49: If the shoe fits, wear it.

Youth shoe sizes go up to size 6 Youth (6Y). This is equivalent to up to a size 8 adult women's shoe size. I wear a women's size 7, therefore this size converts to a size 5 youth. I recently purchased two pair of youth Adidas athletic running shoes on sale for $19.95 each. Similar styled shoes were found in the women's section for over $45 each.

Tip #50: Shop at outlet stores.

Malls are more expensive because stores have to support greater overhead expenses. Outlet malls have many of the same stores and have reduced prices because they carry merchandise that is from a past season or two.

Tip #51: The two drink minimum.

Have you ever gone to a performance or venue that requires you to purchase two drinks at a minimum? If you are there with a partner that means 4 high priced drinks! Save on your drink bill by ordering juice or soda. It's not mandatory that you have to purchase alcoholic beverages.

Tip #52: Avoid shopping with your kids.

Need I say more? Kids of all ages make you spend more money by their sheer presence. They also cause you to spend more time in the store which increases your chances of spending more money. Avoid shopping with the kids by any means necessary.

Tip #53: Give family gifts on holidays.

Instead of giving individual gifts to members of a family group (i.e. your bother-in-law, his spouse, and their 2 children) give a family gift such as gift card to a family friendly restaurant or a collector's edition of a family board game. You spend less time in the store and you save money by combining several gifts into one.

Tip #54: Just say no.

This phrase was made famous in the 80's by former President Ronald Reagan's drug-free campaign. But it can be used in your goals to become debt free and grow your savings. Just say no. It takes practice, but the more you practice it, the better it will feel when you get closer to your goals.

Tip #55: Ask the cashier for discounts.

Sometimes the cashiers have a master coupon code or extra coupons that were left from previous customers and all you have to do is ask. Asking if they have any coupons or discounts that apply could save you 10%, 20%, or even 30% on your purchase.

Tip #56: Clearance racks.

This is my mom's hardest thing to do. She says that items look different or cheaper when they are on the clearance racks. On a couple of our shopping occasions I have purposely pointed out purchases that she has made, and how much she could have saved now that the item is on sale or on the clearance rack. I've also taken it a step further and purchased the same item from the clearance rack as she did and it looked just as good.

Head straight for the clearance racks to find the best deals. You may have to hunt a little more to find your items, but when you find your items they are often 50-80% off the original price.

Tip #57: Give to get.

Several stores offer discount coupons with great savings if you donate an item such as a coat or other clothing. Donate your lightly used goods to get the discounts on a newer purchase. Giving to charitable organizations can also get you a tax credit which may help you with your itemized deductions on your yearly taxes.

Tip #58: Do not go to the grocery store hungry.

Most of us know the philosophy of going to the grocery store hungry, you end up spending more. This is true, but how many of us have time to prepare a meal before grocery shopping? Not many. Use the store's deli or produce section to your advantage. Grab a small portion of food from the deli or a piece of fruit before starting your grocery shopping. Just this little bit of food can save you from putting several items that you would only buy because you were hungry in your cart.

Tip #59: Use coupons.

I do not recommend subscribing to newspapers because most of the articles are available online on the newspaper's website. I do suggest that you purchase the Sunday paper from a dollar store because they have valuable store coupons. You can invest $1 and often get savings of $8-10 for groceries, home and beauty products, and even clothing. Coupons can also be found in Valu-Paks, single mailers, and online at coupon websites. Combine coupons with store sales for greater savings. I always receive $5 off a purchase of $10 or more coupons from a local beauty store. I purchase my favorite lip gloss this way. The lip gloss retails for $8.50 per tube. Occasionally the store has a buy one, get one ½ off sale on this lip gloss. I purchase two lip glosses on sale for $8.50 and $4.25 (1/2 off), and then I apply my $5 off coupon bringing my total to only $ 7.75. I got two lip glosses for less than I would pay for one.

Be careful to stick to the items on the coupons. If you go in the store to purchase items from a coupon and you end up spending money on other items not on sale then you didn't save any money.

Chapter 4

Tip #60: Do your own hair.

Take the time to learn your hair and how to manage it. Learning to do your own hair tasks such as trimming ends, coloring, blow drying and styling, can save you hundreds of dollars a year. There are multiple videos and photos online that instruct you how to do these different hair tasks.

Tip #61: Sell unused items.

EBay, Amazon, and Craigslist are all user-friendly websites that help you unload unwanted and unused items. If you look around your house you probably have several items that you no longer use or need that other people are looking to purchase. Some examples of items that are easy to sell on sites such as these are cell phones (even broken ones), cameras, video games, electronics, purses, shoes, and clothing.

Tip #62: Sell yourself!

Many of us work 9 to 5's, but we have great skills in other areas. Are you great with computers? Can you change the oil or brakes on a car? Can you type a great letter or email? These are skills that others may not be so great in. Start charging for your skills and earn extra money on the side.

Tip #63: Be Crafty.

You don't have to be an artistic person to be creative. You just have to think outside the box. When I look at an item in a store, I always think about what it is intended to be used for, but I also think about what else it can be used for. I think about what its original color is, but also what it would look like as another color. I often use fabric, a staple gun, or spray paint to change an item from one look to a completely different look.

Tip #64: Open your mail.

Mail that is often perceived as "junk mail" sometimes has great deals, special offers, and coupons. All of the mail can get overwhelming, so create a strategy of opening, reading, saving or discarding your mail.

Tip #65: Free samples.

Ask for free samples at stores that sell products. Companies send samples to stores to give out, but customers rarely ask. So when a customer finally asks for samples they hand them a ton of them. Samples are a great way to try products before committing fully to them.

Tip #66: Use discount programs.

Sign up for discount programs from frequent flyer programs, hotels, car rental, and restaurants. The points add up and can be used for free flights, hotel rooms, car rentals, and meals. My husband and I seek out and stay at the same hotel brand and have earned enough points for frequent free nights, express check-ins, and even restaurant gift cards.

Tip #67: Use plastic.

Use plastic flowers. Flowers are a great way to add color and texture to your space. There are high quality flowers also known as silk flowers and greenery. Use them to decorate indoors and outdoors. I use the silk flowers and greenery in my outdoor porch urns and throughout our house.

Tip #68: Garage and moving sales.

These are great opportunities to find needed items for reasonable prices. Power tools, yard tools, appliances, children's items, collector's items, furniture and electronics are many of the items that can be found at garage and moving sales. Remember that even if an item has a price sticker on it everything is usually negotiable.

Tip #69: Use your network.

Use your social and professional network to get perks. Through your network you can find event tickets, comedy shows, great seats at upscale restaurants, and discounts at various places. You can post through your social network sites a wanted request for these things, or you can barter services for these things also.

Tip #70: Take advantage of flexible spending accounts.

Many companies offer flexible spending accounts (FSA) as a part of their benefits packages. Flexible spending accounts allow you to contribute a part of your payroll dollars into an account pre-taxed and then use that account to pay for healthcare related expenses such as co-pays, deductibles, prescriptions, and over-the-counter drugs. One of the hidden benefits is that you can use it to pay for massages and facials from certified providers. My husband and I currently have a membership at a certified massage provider and we each receive a relaxing one hour massage once a month courtesy of our flexible spending account. Love it!

Tip #71: If it's broke, fix it.

I love my mom, bless her heart. She has taught me an abundance of great things in life. However, she taught me one bad habit that was hard on my pockets and hard to break. If I had something and it broke, it was considered useless and I threw it away. There was no attempt to repair it, repurpose it, or gain any benefit from items, pieces, or parts. I just threw it away and bought a new one. But during my monetary coming of age, I learned to not consider an item useless or trash-worthy until you exhausted all reasonable repair or repurposing efforts; and even after those efforts if the item is made of metal (i.e. a broken bicycle, lock safe without a combination) it still has value as recyclable metal.

Tip #72: Use free bill pay from your bank.

Bill pay is offered for free by most large banking institutions. It is a great way to pay most of your bills from a checking or savings account. One trick my husband and I do with bill pay is to divide our bills into 4 payments. My husband receives his pay direct deposit on the opposite weeks I receive my pay by direct deposit. Therefore I set up bill pay to pay our bills every week. For example, our budgeted electric bill is $160 per month. Bill pay sends $40 from each direct deposit to our electricity provider. We do the same for most of our other bills; Allowing us to manage many bills by breaking them down into smaller payments.

Tip #73: Have sex!!!

Studies show that sex relieves stress, and with stress relieved you feel satisfied and are less likely to participate in activities (i.e. compulsive shopping) that give temporary satisfaction.

Tip #74: Look at your savings as a yearly number.

When reviewing your budget and your spending for areas where you can save, look at the savings as a yearly total. For example, when reviewing your cell phone bill you may save money by reducing your plan or going to another provider. If the savings will be $34 a month, this is $408 a year.

Tip #75: Collect and use loose change.

Many men already participate in this action often. It's as simple as taking the change that you get from a purchase and placing it in a container. However, many times people collect and collect the change but never apply it towards anything. Make a goal for the change. Collect it for a year, and use it to pay your insurance premiums for the year (saving more money by paying for the entire year in a lump sum), paying down a credit card, Christmas shopping, or starting an Individual Retirement Account or College Savings Account.

Tip #76: Return purchases to get cash back or store credit.

Have you ever purchased an item you didn't use, it didn't fit, or you simply didn't like it after you got it home? We all have; but many have just accepted the loss. Start the habit of returning the items to the store for your money back, or at minimum a store credit to use towards something you can now use.

Tip #77: Do your homework.

Before you commit to a large purchase do your homework and research the facts about the item to include consumer reports on quality and reliability, maintenance and repair costs, resale value, and whether or not you can find the item somewhere else for less money. A few extra clicks of your mouse can save you big money.

Tip #78: Get rid of your home phone.

Land lines are becoming obsolete, and are no longer required for the operation of phone-based services. Home security systems, internet service, and fax machines now can be controlled through wireless services. Most adults have a cell phone and use it as their primary source of contact, thus a home phone is an added bill that could save you hundreds of dollars a year if you got rid of it. My husband and I have not had a home phone in over 7 years, and we both operate home-based businesses.

Tip #79: Have ATM envy.

You hear it all the time that you should avoid using non-network ATMs. One swipe a week at another bank's ATM can cost you hundreds of dollars a year.

Two smarter ideas would be to get cash back at a store you are making a purchase at, or to make a really small purchase (i.e. a fifty-cent pack of gum), and get cash back at a convenience store for no charge.

Tip #80: Only get the cash you need.

My husband had a habit of only needing a certain amount of cash, lets say $20, but would withdraw $40-60 from the ATM. Can you guess what happened? He would find something to spend the additional $20-40 on just because he had it. This adds up over time and you could end up wasting thousands of dollars a year by doing this. Only withdraw or get cash back for the amount you truly need.

Tip #81: Buy used appliances.

Through word of mouth, used appliance vendors, or classified ads on sites such as Craigslist.com or Pennysaver.com you can locate individuals selling quality used appliances. When my husband and I bought our house all the appliances were negotiated into the sales contract, but at the last minute the seller took the washer and dryer out of the sale. So within 4-5 days of closing we were in need of a washer and dryer. We were able to locate a washer through a small resale vendor, and the dryer was given to us by a relative. When the dryer was at the end of its life cycle we returned to the resale vendor and purchased a reasonable dryer at a fraction of the cost of a new one. To date we have done hundreds of loads of laundry on both the used washer and dryer.

Tip #82: Use free Smartphone apps.

Download smart phone applications that are free. The free versions of many of the apps contain banner advertisements, but they function just as the full paid versions do. You can also download apps that alert you when the full paid versions of apps are now free.

Tip #83: Do not procrastinate.

If you become aware of savings through a commercial, a mailer, or word-of-mouth follow-up right away by doing your research to validate the savings and make the change right away. Too many people hear of savings, but procrastinate on doing their research and making the change and they take months before taking advantage of the savings. Companies love procrastinators and they make millions of dollars off of their lack of follow-through.

Tip #84: Get rid of duplicate items sooner than later.

Wii, Playstations, and Nintendo consoles are taking the place of DVD players by allowing owners to stream unlimited movies and TV shows through them. Cell phones are taking the place of digital cameras and individual GPS units. These duplicate items should be sold as soon as they are no longer used at a relative frequency. Sell them sooner while they still have value because as they become obsolete to more and more households their value will decrease significantly.

Tip #85: Ask for prescription samples.

Doctors and healthcare providers have samples of many of the drugs they prescribe to patients. If the doctor prescribes you a medication ask if he/she has samples of the drug. Many times they do and they give you enough to solve the ailment. It never hurts to ask.

Tips #86: If you don't want to do it, don't do it.

Since the beginning of friendships, friends are great at pressuring us at doing and buying things we don't want to do or need. Build courage and start practicing saying no. One of the worst feelings you can have is not liking something and knowing that you are paying your hard earned money to not like it.

Tip #87: Stay organized.

Minimal organization is key to many of the creative tips listed in this book. Keep receipts in one location, keep coupons with you, and make a plan to review your mail regularly keeping what you need and discarding what you don't. These are just a few of the ideas that will help you stay organized, which can position you to focus better on making great saving decisions.

Tip #88: Take care of what you already have.

A great way to save is to not duplicate purchases due to lack of care or proper maintenance. Follow the proper care instructions on products to get the full product lifeline and sometimes even longer.

Tip #89: Do not loan money, give it.

The first rule of thumb is to not loan money that you cannot afford to receive back. If you are using your bill money or money that you require to keep yourself afloat, do not loan it. However, if all of your obligations are met and you still have money left over, I suggest that you give it rather than lend it. The second rule of thumb is that money and friendships (this includes family) do not mix. If someone asks to borrow money from us, we rarely loan them all that they ask for, but we generally GIVE them less than what they have asked for. We also let them know that the money is a gift and not a loan.

Tip #90: Use student loans.

One loan that I do not consider bad debt is the student loan. However, I must put a disclaimer on this tip and state that if you use the student loans you must complete the educational program and earn your degree. Higher education is what is and will continue to be needed to be competitive within the workforce. Therefore the student loan is one loan that may be necessary to improve your job prospects.

Tip #91: If you have to borrow, borrow from yourself.

If you have to purchase something that is beyond what you can afford from your paycheck then you should borrow the money from your own savings or 401(k). This is based on your ability to pay your savings or 401(k) back within a reasonable amount of time such as 6-18 months. Do not borrow money to incur more negative debt, or to purchase items that are wanted rather than needed.

Tip #92: Be on time.

Do you often arrive at your destination late? Work hard to change this bad habit. Arriving late can cost you money because you probably burning more gas by punching on the gas petal trying to make up time, not to mention putting yourself at higher risk for traffic violations and accidents. By arriving early or at least being on time you may get a chance to network and when you network you often learn of great opportunities that could increase your finances or save you more money.

Tip #93: You set the standard.

Everyone's heard of "keeping up with the Joneses". You need to reinvent this concept and create your own standard of living based on own your income, family dynamic, and priorities. We often tell our children to become leaders and not followers. Therefore, we need to take our own advice and be leaders and controllers of our own financial destiny. The phrase should now state, "keeping up with the _____ (fill in the blank with your last name)".

Tip #94: Rent out items.

You can rent items that you own that you are not using to others that need to use them temporary. Everything from barbeque grills, power tools, shop vacs, coolers, ladders, storage space, bicycles, sports or camping equipment, cars, boats, and motorcycles can be rented out to others for temporary use. Websites such as Loanables.com and snapgoods.com list your items for rent and give you protection guarantee for your items.

Tip #95: Split your direct deposit.

First, start by setting a primary direct deposit account with your employer for your paycheck. Second, add a secondary deposit account at a banking institution such as a credit union that you do not have quick access to. Deposit a majority of your pay into your primary account for your bills and monthly living costs, and deposit a set amount based on your saving goals and abilities into the second account. Since you purposely do not have quick access to the second account you will probably not access often allowing you to meet your savings goals and commitments.

Tip #96: Use no contract services.

Research and find services that do not require a contract such as cell phones, fitness clubs, security systems, and others. Contracts lock you into payments for extended periods of time and often have cancellation fees that are equivalent to the remainder of the contract.

Tip #97: Use pre-paid debit cards.

Use a pre-paid debit card for payments that require automatic debit deductions from a checking or savings account. I do not recommend using them for daily regular purchases because they have hefty usage fees. However, for the protection of your primary accounts and to allow you to remain in control of your payments use the pre-paid debit cards for these types of set-ups.

Tip #98: Do not overdraft your accounts.

Avoid overdrafts by any means necessary. An average bank overdraft fee is $37.50. Although banking reform is changing how many overdraft fees accounts are charged, just one is still too many. Set your account up to decline any charges that cause your account to go into a negative balance. In addition, although most people now use debit cards for purchases, you should still balance your account regularly to avoid negative balances before they occur.

Tip #99: 7-7-7

Pick 4, PowerBall, scratch-off lottery tickets, casino slot machines, and the list goes on are all good ways to waste money. The odds of winning may increase from game to game, but overall gambling is designed for the house to win, and win more often than you do. So if you are playing the lottery or gambling hoping to win big so you can pay off all your bills, your chances of paying the bills off are greater if you learn ways to save money and apply those savings to the debt, than gambling, losing, and becoming more indebted.

Additionally, the money you lose goes to pay for several things that your tax dollars already pay for. So you are essentially double taxing yourself.

Tip #100: Invest in single stocks.

There are several companies that advertise the purchase and trade of stocks online, and they come with a requirement of a minimum $1000 initial investment and a list of purchase and trading fees. However, there are several smaller sites in which you can purchase individual stocks with no minimum requirements or large purchase fees.

Tip #101: Don't ask. Don't tell.

If someone compliments your belongings, items you just purchased, your home décor, clothing, or simply your great style and believes you paid a great deal of money on it, let them. However, if someone asks where they can find a better deal on a product or service you should share your experience with them, it will give you pleasure knowing that you saved someone else their hard earned money also.

About the Author

LISA EVANS holds a Masters of Business Administration degree from American Intercontinental University and has been working in Human Resources for over twelve years. Lisa began practicing her frugal ways when her family relocated to the Chicagoland area and had to adjust to the higher cost of living. She is also the author of "After the Dance, 60 Real Life Tips to Help You Create a Healthy and Happy Marriage". Lisa, her husband, and their son reside in Country Club Hills, Illinois.

www.ingramcontent.com/pod-product-compliance
Lightning Source LLC
Chambersburg PA
CBHW030816180526
45163CB00003B/1313